D1610734

# HOW TO DRAW
# A RHINOCEROS

X400 000018 5297

# How to
# Draw
# a
# Rhinoceros

poems Kate Sutherland

Canada Council for the Arts    Conseil des Arts du Canada    Funded by the Government of Canada    Financé par le gouvernement du Canada    |  Canada

ONTARIO ARTS COUNCIL
CONSEIL DES ARTS DE L'ONTARIO
an Ontario government agency
un organisme du gouvernement de l'Ontario

The production of this book was made possible through the generous assistance of the Canada Council for the Arts and the Ontario Arts Council. BookThug also acknowledges the support of the Government of Canada through the Canada Book Fund and the Government of Ontario through the Ontario Book Publishing Tax Credit and the Ontario Book Fund.

*Library and Archives Canada Cataloguing in Publication*

Sutherland, Kate, 1966–, author
How to draw a rhinoceros / Kate Sutherland.

Poems.
Issued in print and electronic formats.
ISBN 978-1-77166-260-4 (paperback)
ISBN 978-1-77166-261-1 (html)
ISBN 978-1-77166-262-8 (pdf)
ISBN 978-1-77166-263-5 (kindle)

I. Title.

PS8587.U795H68 2016        C811'.6        C2016-905012-2
                                            C2016-905013-0

cover image by Kate Bergin: *The Company of Unlikely Travellers*, oil on canvas

PRINTED IN CANADA

CONTENTS

# A NATURAL HISTORY OF THE RHINOCEROS

A nose-horned beast
strange and never seen in our country
a very wonderful creature
entirely different from what we fancied

In its fifth month, not much bigger than a large dog
At two years, no taller than a young heifer
but broader, thicker, jutting out at the sides
like a cow with calf
Large as a horse, not much larger
than the bounding oryx, bigger than a bull
Equal to an elephant in length but
lower to the ground. Like a wild boar
in outward form and proportion, especially its mouth
A mouth not unlike the proboscis of an elephant
the underlip like that of an ox, the upper like that of a horse
tongue soft and smooth as a dog's
Piglike head, eyes the shape of a hog's, ears like a donkey's
Skin the colour of an elephant's, two girdles hanging down
like dragons' wings

Dark red head, blue eyes, white body
On its back, dense spots showing darkly
purple spots upon a yellow ground
Red hairs on its forehead, yellowish brows
Skin the colour of boxwood:
mouse grey, grey brown, blackish brown
dirty brown, dark brown, dark ash
the colour of a toad
the colour of a speckled turtle

It fears neither the claws of the tiger
nor the weapons of the huntsman
its hide impervious to darts
so thick as to be impenetrable by a Japanese dagger

Lead musket balls flatten on impact
It does not feel the sting of flies
Dry, hard skin, four fingers thick
studded with scales, like a coat of mail, loricated like armour
covered in calluses resembling clothes buttons
Extravagant skin, loose like so much coach leather
lying upon the body in folds. Between the folds
smooth and soft as silk

The horn stands upon the nose of the animal
as upon a hill, rises dread and sharp
as hard as iron, a little curved up
sometimes three-and-a-half feet long
The base is purest white, the sharp point
flaming crimson, the middle black
The colour of the horn is various:
black, white, sometimes ash-coloured
Commonly these horns are brown or olive-coloured
yet some are grey and even white

There is another horn not upon the nose
but upon the withers

Small piercing eyes, red eyes
dull sleepy eyes
that seldom open completely
eyes in the very centre of the cheeks
eyes placed as low down as the jaws
eyes so small placed so low and so obliquely
they have little vivacity and motion
eyes that only see sideways
eyes that only see straight ahead

Teeth broad and deep in its throat
teeth so sharp, they cut straw and tree branches
like a pair of scissors
two strong incisive teeth to each jaw

twenty-four smaller teeth
six on each side of each jaw

It will kill with licking
and by the roughness of its tongue
lay bare the bones
No animal near its size has so soft a tongue
it feels like passing the hand over velvet

Strong legs as big around as a man's waist
massive legs terminating in large feet
each foot divided into three great claws

Sprouting from its slender inconsiderable tail
black shining hairs a foot long
the thickness of shoemaker's thread
not round like other hair but flattish
like little pieces of whalebone

All the breed are males
and a female is never seen
The penis is an extraordinary shape
The female is the same in all respects
except the sex. The female has two teats
and an udder. The female brings forth
but one young. The male horn is harder
and sharper than the female's
The male has a small extra horn
on its back right shoulder

It never attacks men unless provoked
but then becomes formidable
If it meets a man in a red coat, it will rush him
and throw him over its head with such violence
the fall alone is fatal

It can reach an age of a hundred years
It is probable that it lives as a man, seventy or eighty years
It seldom lives beyond twenty

No creature that pursues it can overtake it
It falls asleep before virgins and then
can easily be taken and carried away
Attack it during hot weather when it is lying in the marsh
Cover a pit with green branches on the path
from the forest to the riverside
Destroy the old ones with firearms
If there happens to be a cub
seize and tame it
Take it by gunfire

## HOW TO DRAW A RHINOCEROS

Begin with an elephant. Shorten the legs and the nose, pin back the ears
To cement the distinction, assert eternal enmity between the animals

*Compare to*:
cow  calf  bull  ox
oryx  buffalo  camel
horse  donkey  goat  lamb
lynx  lion
pig  hog  boar  sow  swine
dog  rabbit  mouse
eagle  duck
tortoise  turtle  toad
dragon  elephant
overturned coach
mountain

*Distinguish from*:
fox
tiger
elephant
hippopotamus
unicorn

Use a woolly rhinoceros skull to sculpt a dragon's head

Delete all rhinoceros references from the Bible
Replace with unicorns

Add a dorsal horn and a suit of armour

Incorporate its image into an apothecary's coat of arms

Put a jaunty human skeleton in front
and one behind

Sketch a front view, a back view, a side view. Inset details
of horn, hoofs, ears, nose, tail, each of its component parts

Liken its genitalia to botanical specimens with Latin names:
e.g., *Digitalis floribus purpureis, Aristolochia floribus purpureis*, &c

Picture it grazing placidly in the foreground, while a fearsome compatriot
gores an elephant in the background

Position it on an island under a palm tree
in a jungle draped with vines
in a marsh rolling in mud
next to a river
in a desert
on a cliff edge

Depict it stalked by an Indian swordsman, or African tribesmen
armed with bows and arrows. Don't be afraid to mix and match

Confuse its armour with an armadillo's and situate it in the Americas

Render it with a ring through its nose, being led by a chain
or with its legs shackled

Paint it lying on its side, feeding in its pen
preening before an audience. Divest it of its horn
Mask the audience. Make *it* realistic
the audience fantastical

Sculpt it from marble. Cast it in bronze. Model it in porcelain
Perch a turbaned Turk on its back
Place a robed mandarin cross-legged at its feet
Put a clock in its belly

Enamel it on a serving plate

Engrave its likeness on a medal, a series of medals
suitable for collecting

Emblazon it together with a sailor on a banner
the sailor raising a glass of beer
in a toast: *Bon voyage!*

## DÜRER'S RHINOCEROS

I.

In the year our living such a marvel I had to send you this
representation made after toad protected scales large as this comes
to fight first whets horn pushing his forelegs then rips open where
skin thinnest therefore fears the rhinoceros he always gores him
whenever he meets an elephant

II.

It is said that great powerful Emanuel represented here complete
form live speckled tortoise covered thick plates like its legs almost
invulnerable begins sharpening rocks obstinate frightened when it
encounters stomach throttles down its front legs cannot fend off
fast cunning so there is nothing it can do

## ELEPHANT V. RHINOCEROS

### I. Witnesses

Ctesias, physician
Artemidorus Ephesius, geographer
Diodorus Siculus, historian
Oppian, poet
Pliny, scientist and historian
Valentin Ferdinand, printer
Albrecht Dürer, artist
Guillaume de Salluste du Bartas, poet
Edward Topsell, naturalist
Oliver Goldsmith, novelist
Commodore George Anson
Captain Thomas Williamson

Jean Chardin, traveller
Comte de Buffon, naturalist
John Church, physician
Stephani Polito, menagerist
Richard Owen, anatomist

## II. Opening Arguments

The rhinoceros is especially hostile to the elephant
There is a natural antipathy
      a natural enmity between the beasts
The rhinoceros is a natural-born enemy of the elephant
It is the elephant's inveterate
                  sworn
                  fierce
                  deadly
                  mortal enemy

              No antipathy has been observed between these animals
                    In captivity, they live quietly together
                        without offence or provocation

The rhinoceros prepares itself for combat by sharpening its horn against
            gets ready for battle by filing its horn on
Before attacking, it sharpens
               always first whets its horn upon the stones
                        against a rock

The rhinoceros attacks
        surprises
        opens the fight with
        overcomes the elephant by

charging it at the chest
thrusting its forehead under the belly
fastening its horn in the lower part of the elephant's belly
In the encounter it strikes the elephant on the chest
        runs at the elephant with his head between his forelegs
          slips under
          goes especially for
          strikes most of all at the belly
          shoves its horn in the stomach

which it knows to be softer
           the softest part
                tenderest and most penetrable part
                weakest part of the body
                thinnest skin
                where his sharpened blade will in


           As the rhinoceros is naturally of a pacific temper
it is probable that accounts of it engaging the elephant
                              are without foundation


The rhinoceros rips open the flesh with its horn as a sword
           rips up the elephant's belly
           tears it to pieces
                without mercy
           gores him
           wounds mortally
           opens his guts

The elephant's entrails tumble out


                    The rhinoceros has no taste for flesh

III. Physical Evidence

The elephant is often found dead in the forests pierced
with the horn of a rhinoceros
elephants are occasionally found dead
obviously from wounds given by the rhinoceros

> A rhinoceros dead at the London Zoo
> seventh rib fractured by an elephant
> poking its tusks through the palings
> between their enclosures
> death ascribed to injury of the left lung
> caused by the fracture

IV. Eyewitness Accounts

*Lisbon, 1515*
Valentin Ferdinand:
On the day of the Blessed Trinity
an elephant was led to a courtyard
near the King's Palace
A rhinoceros was led to the same place
The elephant uneasy and furious
uttered a tremendous cry, ran
to one of the barred windows
wrenched the iron bars
with trunk and teeth
fled away

*Persia, 1667*
Jean Chardin:
On the left of the Royal stables
were two great elephants
covered with cloths of gold brocade
and one rhinoceros
so near one to the other
The animals showed not the least
aversion or uneasiness

*Africa, 1807*
Captain Thomas Williamson:
The late Major Lally witnessed
a most desperate engagement
between a rhinoceros
and a large, male elephant
the latter protecting a small herd
retiring in a state of alarm
The elephant was worsted
and fled into heavy jungle

*London, 1814*
Stephani Polito:
The formidable rhinoceros
one of the largest ever seen
In the adjoining den, in the same apartment
a fine large male elephant
adorned with long ivory tusks
The two animals so closely united
so reconciled
as to take their food from each other

V. Closing Arguments

The rhinoceros kills the elephant
            kills many of them
many a time it lays so mighty a beast dead in the dust

        unless the rhinoceros is prevented by the trunk and tusks
    the elephant may defend itself with the trunk or teeth then
                    throw the rhinoceros down
                        throw it on the ground
                                and kill it

                the elephant succumbing to the pain drops
                        and crushes its enemy
                    by the weight of its body

    seldom does combat cease without death of both fighters

The rhinoceros gores the elephant and carries him off upon his
head, but the blood and fat of the elephant run into his eyes, and
make him blind; he falls to the ground; and what is very astonish-
ing, the roc carries them both away in her claws, to be meat for her
young ones

ACCORDING TO THE APOTHECARY

Prescribe unicorn horn for
poisons and malignant evils bites
of mad dogs and scorpions coughs
pestilent fevers all distempers
proceeding from a cold cause
fainting fits convulsions
children's ailments including
colic and worms fluxes
obstructions cramps
ulcers heartburn
running gout impotence
the pox sore eyes corns
the Kings Evil dropsy
epilepsy consumption
proliferation of vermin
the plague rabies
rickets scurvy
the green sickness
palpitations of the heart
loss of memory
melancholy or sadness

Prescribe rhinoceros horn for
poison snakebites overdoses
colds laryngitis typhoid
intermittent fevers other
distempers delirium dizziness
faintings convulsions
infantile convulsions and spasms
food poisoning dysentery
violent vomiting
nosebleeds headaches
gout arthritis rheumatism
blurry vision boils
carbuncles dermatitis
strokes facial paralysis
high blood pressure
smallpox cancer comas
brain haemorrhages
insanity devil possession
bewitching nightmares
hallucinations miasmas
melancholia fear and anxiety

Continuous administration
prevents diseases and infections
by fortifying the noble parts
preserves vigour and a good
complexion to old age whitens
the teeth prolongs youth
makes the barren fertile
overcomes feminine modesty

There are many ways to prepare it
Make the horn into a cup
and drink from it
Scrape powder from the horn
and dissolve in water or wine
Mix with oil to make a salve
Wrap the powder in silk
and cast it in water
Form it into pills

The horn may be mingled with
other medicines
A powerful antidote to poison
is composed of
unicorn's horn musk amber
gold and pearls

Continuous administration
destroys malignant acids
which stir up pernicious diseases
builds energy and makes one
robust nourishes the blood
calms the liver keeps one
young and potent
forever elevates the libido

There are many ways to prepare it
Make a goblet from the horn
and drink from it
Mix shavings of horn
with water or wine
Grind the shavings into a paste
Put the powder in a muslin bag
and boil in a cup of water
Manufacture it into tablets

The horn may be mingled with
other medicines
The most popular remedy
is a medicine ball made from
rhinoceros horn musk herbs
and cow gallstones

The rest of the animal is also potent
Make an ointment of unicorn liver
and egg yolk to treat leprosy
Wear shoes of its leather
to assure healthy feet thighs
and joints
Gird the body with a belt cut
from its hide
to avert attack by plague or fever

Whether in the piece or powdered
it must be fresh. Over time
unicorn horn loses its virtue

The rest of the animal is also potent
Cook rhinoceros liver with spices
and eat to cure tuberculosis
Use its skin and tallow
to treat swelling and stiffness
in the joints
Carve a ring from its smallest
bone and wear
to ward off evil spirits

A freshly killed male rhinoceros
is best. Most dependable
is the horn of a young calf

# RHINOCEROS ODYSSEY

*August 1738*
She's orphaned
in Assam
at 2 months
raised in the home of a director
of the Dutch East India Company
dines off fine china plates
charms children
and house guests

*November 1740*
sold to sea captain
Douwe Mout van der Meer

Calcutta to Rotterdam
8,840 nautical miles
aboard the *Knappenhof*
bowls of beer above deck
an occasional puff of tobacco
from the captain's pipe
protected from sun by a canvas shade
from dry, salt air by a coat of fish oil
from malnutrition by oranges
peel and all

three years old
3,000 lbs
5 feet high

*1742*
already a pin-up
in Leiden bookshops
before her first public appearance
thanks to a Jan Wandelaar woodcut:
*Human Skeleton and Young Rhinoceros*

*1746*
in a barn on the outskirts
she squeaks, snorts, snores
daily eats 60 lbs of hay, 20 lbs of bread
drinks 14 buckets of water
prepares for travel

an army of carpenters, locksmiths
blacksmiths, wheelwrights
is required to craft a travelling coach
for this zaftig Cinderella
8 horses to pull it
20 over poor roads

handbills and broadsides
announce her arrival in the next town:
*Consider this animal you see before you*
*and ask yourself, do you not strive to search*
*day and night for God's miraculous might*
*in the book of nature? The eye stares*
*in amazement, the mouth must freely admit:*
*God is as mighty as he is wonderful!*
*God made it so man can delight in it*

in town for 12 days
viewing hours: 9–noon & 2–6
4 groschen for a glimpse
half a gulden for a closer look
*persons of rank can pay*
*according to their desire*

souvenirs for sale
half a gulden for a large engraving
2 groschen for the small one with the Indian

*The 'Dutch' Rhinoceros in Hanover*
watercolour
by G.L. Scheitz

she's truly launched
among the fish stalls
of Berlin's Spittel markt

*Guest Book*
*April 26, 1746*
Frederick the Great of Prussia: "Worth every one of the 18 Ducats
    I paid."
Pierre Louis Maupertuis, president of the Royal Academy of
    Sciences: "Proves the existence of God (& my theory of the
    principle of least action)."
Voltaire, author & philosopher: "*They have found God in the folds
    of the skin of the rhinoceros; one could, with equal reason, deny
    His existence because of the tortoise shell.*"

*September 1746*
broadside revised in Breslau:
*All animal lovers!*
*A living RHINOCEROS has arrived.*
*See the beast which many believe to be*
*the Behemoth of the book of Job*
*See the beast which many have thought apocryphal*
*until now*

*October 1746*
enters Vienna
8 swordsmen striding
alongside the 8 horses
that draw her wagon

on display
in the Freyung
amidst aristocrats

*Guest Book*
*November 5, 1746*
Maria Theresa Hapsburg, Holy Roman Empress: "Very
    educational. Young Karl Joseph was besotted."
Francis I of Lorraine, Holy Roman Emperor: "Ditto."
Karl Joseph, Archduke: "!"

*November 1746*
the Emperor
bestows a baronetcy
on van der Meer
*for the merit of the beast*

8 years old
5,000 lbs
5 feet, 7 inches high
12 feet long
12 feet in circumference

*Guest Book*
*March 1747*
Regensburg
J.M. Barth: "Clearly the Behemoth of the Old Testament."
J. Reinhard: "Blasphemy!"

*April 1747*
Freiberg, near Dresden
shining at the Wiesemann Inn
of the Golden Star

*Guest Book*
*April 19, 1747*
Johann Kaendler, animal modeller, Meissen porcelain factory: "It
    appears that Dürer took some liberties…"
Augustus III, Elector of Saxony & King of Poland: "I want one of
    those in porcelain. Life-size."

*Sultan on a Rhinoceros*
painted porcelain mounted on a Louis XV base
by Johann Kaendler

*April 1747*
Leipzig
Easter Fair

*Guest Book*
Friedrich Gotthilf Freytag, classicist: "A pleasure to see the animal
    of which Pliny and his fellow Romans wrote so eloquently."
Christian Fürchtegott Gellert, poet & the German Aesop: "Wrote
    a poem about an old man I met in the line-up. Gave the
    rhinoceros a cameo."

*July 1747*
a month in the country
at the pleasure of the Landgrave of Hesse-Kassel
she's given the run
of the Orangery, an oasis of humid air
and citrus scents
in return she provides
mountains of dung
to fertilize rare botanical specimens
and serves as a symbol of strength
potent as her host's
statue of Hercules

*November 1747*
Mannheim
preening at the Peacock Inn

*Guest Book*
*November 20, 1747*
Carl Theodor, Elector Palatine: "Got to keep up with the
    Landgraves…"

boards a barge
a rhinoceros on the Rhine
Germany into Switzerland
an alpine journey worthy
of Hannibal's elephants

*Winter 1748*
Bern, Basel, Zurich
price of admission: 2, 4, or 8 batzen
depending on the view

*Spring 1748*
medals added to the merch table
a selection to please any collector
silver, bronze, pewter
engraved with her current weight
in French, German, or Italian

Horace Mann, baronet & diplomat, to Horace Walpole, Earl of
Orford & member of the British Parliament: *"We are told that
Augustus himself did not disdain to be a Rhinocerontajo by showing
one publickly to the Romans though I have never heard that a medal of
it was struck, as has now been done in honour of this, one of which has
been sent to me, and, which, if it was worthwhile, I would send you to
enrich your cabinet."*

*May 6, 1748*
Stuttgart
publickly weighed
in an ostentatious contraption
of straps and pulleys
and measured
by a nervous bureaucrat
with an impeccable reputation
and an inadequate tape measure

9 years old
5,000 lbs
6 feet high
12 feet long
12 feet in circumference

*June 12, 1748*
Augsburg
drawn from multiple angles
by Johann Elias Ridinger
with lead pencil on blue paper:
*The 'Dutch' Rhinoceros Lying on its Left Side*
*The 'Dutch' Rhinoceros Standing*
*A Sleeping Rhinoceros*
*A Rhinoceros Leaping*

*October 1748*
Würzburg
*Called "Miss Clara"*
watercolour
by court painter
Anton Clemens Lünenschloss

*Guest Book*
*November 1748*
Leiden
Petrus Camper, anatomist: "The horn stands upon the nasal bone,
    not the forehead, and so provides no evidence for the existence
    of unicorns."

*January 1749*
Versailles
guest of Louis XV
temporary centrepiece
of a menagerie
comprised of
a camel, 2 lions, 2 tigers
a pelican, and a seal

the King wishes to keep her but
unaccustomed to paying for his desires
balks at van der Meer's price:
100,000 écus

King's favour lost
they hotfoot it down the road
to Paris, set up a booth
at the St. Germain Fair

viewing hours: 8 AM–8 PM
admission price: 24, 12, or 6 sous
contrary to custom
servants may not enter free
with their masters

*Guest Book*
*February 3, 1749*
Jean-Baptiste Ladvocat, librarian of the Sorbonne: "She's smaller
    than the poster claims—I measure her at 5 feet, 4 inches high;
    10 feet long, and 10 feet in circumference. (Buy my booklet on
    the way out!)"
Giacomo Casanova, author & adventurer: "The beautiful marquise
    had never seen a rhinoceros before, but still ought not to have
    mistaken the ticket taker for the beast. Our apologies!"
Pierre-Claude Nivelle de La Chaussée, playwright: "That monster
    has stolen my audience."

Friedrich Melchior, Baron von Grimm, journalist & art critic, to
Denis Diderot, writer & philosopher: "*All Paris, so easily inebriated
by small objects, is now busy with a kind of animal called rhinoceros.*"

fashionable ladies commence
wearing their hair á la *rhinocéros*
tall, multicoloured feathers as horns
trailing ribbons as tails

*The Rhinoceros*
life-size on a canvas 15 feet long and 10 feet high
by Jean-Baptiste Oudry

*Louis XV bronze and ormolu rhinoceros clock*
by Jean-Joseph Saint-Germain

*Death Report #1*
*May 30, 1749*
lonely and unsated
rampaged through the streets of Lyon
killed 5 or 6 men
died of rage

*Death Report #2*
*November 1749*
Marseilles
drowned
like the Lisbon rhinoceros
when the small vessel piloting her
from quayside to ship
tipped

*Death Report #3*
*January 1750*
Naples
lost at sea
her captain went with her
weighted by his charge
and the bags of gold
she'd made

*The Rhinoceros in its Booth near the Castelnuovo, Naples*
oil on canvas
Neapolitan School

Mann to Walpole: "*Madame Don Philip has brought the mode into Italy of dressing her head à la rhinocéros, which all our ladies follow, so that the preceding mode à la Commetta is only fit for Madame Suaves and such antiquated beauties.*"

arrives in Rome
shortly after the Paris fashion she inspired
but just as Italian ladies sprout horns
hers disappears
official explanation:
*she rubbed it off against her cage*

*Death Report #4*
*June 1750*
Rome
felled
by the mysterious ailment
that took her horn
ticket sales remain brisk

*Death Report #5*
*January 1751*
Venice
slipped into the lagoon
en route from barge to quay
despite a generous reward
efforts to keep her afloat
failed

*sans* horn, she is perhaps
the least exotic creature
in attendance at Venice's
bacchanalian Carnival

*Guest Book*
Marchese Scipione Maffei, historian & writer: "Startled to see *in the hands of its master the horn which fell off last year.*"

Pietro Longhi, painter: "A true rhinoceros, and a conversation piece."
Alessandro Longhi, son of and apprentice to Pietro: "A conversation
    piece, and a true rhinoceros."

*The Exhibition of a Rhinoceros*
oil on canvas
by Pietro Longhi

*The Rhinoceros*
after Pietro Longhi
etching
by Alessandro Longhi

back home in Leiden
van der Meer takes a wife
has a daughter
but continues
peripatetic

Vienna  Prague
Frankfurt  London
Haarlem  Danzig
Crakow

*1754*
Warsaw
she's the warm-up act
before an Italian comedy
light entertainment
for Augustus III's sons

*June 1755*
Copenhagen
near the Vesterport

*This beast consumes daily*
*80 lbs of hay & 30 lbs of bread*

*besides a good quantity of wine*
*and spirituous liquors*
*They keep it in a great cage*
*set on wheels*

18 years old
6,000 lbs
6 feet high
12 feet long
12 feet in circumference

*1758*
London
Lambeth Market

*See the surprising, great*
*and noble animal called Rhinoceros*
*alive*
*the only one of that kind*
*in all Europe*

viewing hours: 8 AM–6 PM
one shilling the first place
and sixpence the second
*It is to be seen in a tent*
*where there is a way for coaches*
*to come up*

*Death Report #6*
*April 14, 1758*
London
died unexpectedly
at the Horse and Groom
may or may not have been stuffed
by a pioneering taxidermist
and continued on tour

## MAGRATH THE GIANT AND THE RHINOCEROS

Cornelius Magrath, aged 18, has been shown
in publick here these last few days
under the title of The Irish Giant
Born in Tipperary in 1736, the present height
of this Youth is so extraordinary
as to admit a man six and a half feet high
with a hat on, to walk under his arm

On view at a hostelry, can be seen
at the Peacock at Charing Cross
for some time exhibited as a show in this city
exhibited in London, Paris, and other European cities

The most extraordinary production of nature
the most stupendous and gigantick form
of a gigantick stature
of a most gigantick stature

A strikingly handsome person
a forbidding countenance
right eyeball protruding and immovable
the left eye turned toward the nose
an ungainly figure, clumsily made
hands as large as a good-sized shoulder of mutton
knock-knees, shoes 15 inches long

Naturalist Giovanni Bianchi
measured him with a cord
and found him to be 7 Parisian feet tall
2 feet taller than the stature of ordinary men
his height was variously estimated at
7'3"  7'5"  7'8"  8'6"
his weight at 350, 420, 450 lbs
his appetite was moderate, he didn't drink
much, only cider

Pietro Longhi painted him
twice the size of the rhinoceros

He returned to Ireland in 1760
after an attack of intermittent fevers
died alone in his Dublin lodgings

Trinity College students stole
his body, a lecture on his dissection
was presented 3 days later
His skeleton is one of the most
treasured possessions
of the Trinity College Museum

*True portrait made by the hand of Pietro Longhi*
*in the year 1757, on commission from the Noble Gentleman*
*Giovanni Grimani dei Servi, Patrician of Venice*

## THE WILD BEAST MEN

I. Gilbert Pidcock (1743–1810)

Started with a single cassowary
and built *the largest collection
of the animal & feathered creation
ever exhibited to the public*:
a zebra, a beaver, a kangaroo
from Botany Bay, an African lion
a Bengal tiger, an emu, an ostrich
two royal crown pigeons
an elephant, a unicorn
aka a rhinoceros

two hundred species in all
displayed in cages lining three rooms
one shilling per room, or all three
for two shillings & sixpence
*one of the most entertaining
promenades in town*

*truly the modern Noah*
and the sort of stand-up fellow
who'd loan a friend £500
to buy a giant's corpse

took out an insurance policy
on an ailing rhinoceros
before taking it on the road
gave the Queen and Princesses
a private viewing, showed it
to the crowds at Ascot
before the beast died
in a caravan near Portsmouth

hurriedly buried it
to dispense with the stench
uncovered it under cover of night
a fortnight later
to preserve the skin and bones

engraved its image on a coin
good for a single admission
to Pidcock's Royal Menagerie
Exeter 'Change, The Strand

## II. George Wombwell (1777–1850)

Traded in a bootmaker's shop
on Monmouth Street
for life as a travelling showman

began with two boa constrictors
bought at the London docks
made his money back and more
showing them at local inns
for a penny a look

Wombwell's Royal Menagerie
hit the road in 1805
not the first, but the biggest
fifteen brightly-painted caravans
to Pidcock's four

the year his elephant died
upon arrival at Bartholomew Fair
his chief rival posted a sign:
*the only living elephant at the fair*
Wombwell countered: *Come see*
*the only dead elephant at the fair!*
and the crowd crushed in

he tried a similar trick
when a rhinoceros died
a month after purchase
*at enormous expense*
stopped in Birmingham
had it stuffed
its remains
remained a draw

he lost a nephew to an elephant
a niece to a tiger
lost the goodwill of the public
pitting his lions against
a pack of bulldogs
Nero swatted them away
Wallace tore them to bits

*Wombwell is undersized in mind*
*as well as form, a weazen*
*sharp-faced man with a skin reddened*
*by more than natural spirits*

but the public came back
they always came back

*no one probably has done so much*
*to forward the study of natural history*
*amongst the masses*

he left a menagerie each
to his wife, a nephew, a niece
as he sleeps in Highgate Cemetery
beneath a stone lion
(Nero or Wallace)
the show goes on

III. Charles Jamrach (1815–1891)

Jamrach & Sons
Ratcliff Highway, East London
museum, bird shop, wild beast mart

in the museum: a stuffed elephant
skins of an owl-parrot and a kiwi
a mummy found in a saltpetre mine
pottery from Incan tombs
clay masks, porcelain dragons
spears, boomerangs, *weapons*
*of every outlandish sort*

but *dealings in arms and curiosities*
*are almost a hobby, their trade*
*is in animals*

Price List (1879): Zebras £150
Camels £20; Giraffes £40; Ostriches £80
Polar Bears £25; Other Bears from £8 to £16
Leopards £20; Lions £100; Tigers £300

rhinoceroses run higher
but often die in transit
the skulls of two
can be seen in the museum

in the little office at the back
the old Windsor chairs
have been occupied
by many a ship's captain selling
by many a royal, an aristocrat
a menagerie-keeper, a circus owner
a zoo official buying

Mr Jamrach is a fine old gentleman
of legendary strength, once
wrestled a tiger unconscious
after it escaped its cage and ran off
with a small boy dangling from its jaws
he paid £300 in damages to the family
then pocketed the same sum from Wombwell
who bought the beast and advertised
*the tiger that swallowed the boy*
*in Ratcliff Highway*
a bronze statue at Tobacco Dock
commemorates the event

Jamrach is commemorated
in a snail named for him
at the British Museum
*Amoria jamrachi*
and a cameo in the novel *Dracula*
as the dealer
who sold the wolf Bersicker
to the London Zoo

## IV. Richard Owen (1804–1892)

As a young anatomist
he took his corpses
wherever he could find them
sometimes buying
from the wild beast men

his wife recalled
a rhinoceros carcass
late of Wombwell's Menagerie
mouldering in the front hall
till she complained of the smell

but once appointed Hunterian Professor
had a monopoly on animal dissection
at the London Zoo
shut out the evolutionists
for decades

when Death visited the zoo
Owen swooped in after
cut up a giraffe, an ostrich
a snake, Tommy the chimpanzee
Jim the rhinoceros

of the latter he exulted in a letter:
*his anatomy will furnish forth*
*an immortal monograph*
and so it did
*On the Anatomy*
*of the Indian Rhinoceros*
*by Professor OWEN*
*Fellow of the Royal Society, Fellow*
*of the Zoological Society, &c*

V. Abraham Dee Bartlett (1812–1897)

Played among the beasts
of the Exeter 'Change menagerie
as a child, took up taxidermy
at twenty-two
won first prize
in the Great Exhibition of 1851
for a series of specimens:
a sleeping Ourang-utang (*Repose*)
a pair of Impeyan Pheasants (*Courtship*)
and a reconstruction
of the Dodo

received a gold watch from Queen Victoria
for his care of her birds
a signed copy of *On the Origin of Species*
from Charles Darwin, hot off the press

Superintendent of the London Zoo
for forty years
strode about Regent Park
in long coat and top hat
an expert on captive animals
less clever with people

if the rhinoceros attacked
its keepers, it was their own fault
for failing to use the safety door
which may or may not have existed
the *Times* couldn't tell
he fired one injured keeper
demoted the other
fought anonymous critics
in the letters pages

when parents complained
of their children's distress
at witnessing snakes gobble white mice
he switched to brown mice

worst
he sold beloved elephant Jumbo
to P.T. Barnum
and America

## VI. Carl Hagenbeck (1844–1913)

*The territory in which*
*an animal emporium*
*must search for its objects*
*encompasses the entire world*

Made his first sale at twelve
transforming a one-eyed alligator
from gift into profit
left school at fifteen
to build his fishmonger father's
sideline menagerie
into an international concern

an Elephant Depot in Ceylon
an animal catching station
in the Sudan
teams of hunters, trappers everywhere
sold rhinoceroses
to the London and Bronx Zoos
sold P.T. Barnum his first giraffe
supplied a thousand dromedaries
to German troops in Africa

patented his *natural-scientific panorama*
animals enclosed by moats
instead of bars, displayed
people
alongside animals
in ethnographic shows

with his wife in the Tierpark Hagenbeck
*the Adam and Eve*
*of an animal paradise*
*on the Banks of the Elbe*

VII. Dan Rice (1823–1900)

*Hero of the Day, the World's Jester*
*the Great Shakespearean Clown*
*the Gentleman, the Scholar, the Poet*
*the Tragedian, the Orator*
*and whilom Preacher, DAN RICE!*

*Jester of all Jesters*
*leaves the audience*
Abraham Lincoln, Walt Whitman
a young Samuel Clemens
*in a perfect roar of delight*

turned animal trainer
taught a dog to add and subtract
a pig to tell time
an elephant to walk a tightrope

traded two trick mules for Old Put
a rhinoceros named for a General
gained new fame *exercising his will*
*over the most obdurate disposition*
*of animal nature*

in the circus ring
Old Put ascended stairs
bellowed on Rice's command
tolled a bell with his horn
on sight of flames
to alert a clown fire department

Old Put drowned
in the Mississippi
went down with his cage
when a steamboat struck
the circus barge

Rice, known for reinvention
began again
stood for Senate, for Congress
declined a run for President
but with top hat and goatee
remains recognizable
as the model
for Uncle Sam

# TRANSACTIONS OF THE LONDON ZOOLOGICAL SOCIETY'S MENAGERIE, 1834–1875

*May 28, 1834*
Indian Rhinoceros
male
purchased from Captain Fergusson for £1050
died November 1849
dissected by Professor Owen
skin mounted and displayed
in the British Museum

*July 5, 1850*
Indian Rhinoceros
young female
purchased for £350
grew a horn of abnormal size and shape
died December 14, 1873

*July 25, 1864*
Indian Rhinoceros
young female
purchased in Calcutta
through Colonel Agnew
Commissioner of Assam
traded in June 1865
to Paris's Jardin des Plantes
for an African elephant

*July 25, 1864*
Indian Rhinoceros
young male
gift of Arthur Grote
tore off his horn in August 1870
attempting to enter enclosure
of female rhinoceros
horn healed and regrew

*September 11, 1868*
Two-horned Rhinoceros
young male
purchased from Carl Hagenbeck for £1000
originally captured in Upper Nubia
first African Rhinoceros
brought to Europe
since Roman times

*February 15, 1872*
Hairy-eared Rhinoceros
female
purchased from William Jamrach for £1250
originally captured near Chittagong
in Eastern Bengal
mired in quicksand
misidentified as Sumatran
till distinguished
by a peculiar fringe of long hairs
along the edges
of her ears

*August 2, 1872*
Sumatran Rhinoceros
old female
purchased from William Jamrach for £600
originally captured
in the Sunghi-nyong district of Malacca
died September 1872
skin and skull sold
stuffed and displayed
at the British Museum

*March 1, 1874*
Javan Rhinoceros
male
purchased from Cross & Jamrach for £800

originally obtained in Indonesia
where on show at tea gardens
in the city of Batavia

*July 14, 1875*
Sumatran Rhinoceros
adult female
purchased from Charles Jamrach for £600

## O'BRIEN'S FOUR SHOWS

Museum! Menagerie!
Caravan! Circus!

The Rhinoceros
or Unicorn of Holy Writ

huge animal
immense size
enormous footprints
prodigious proportions
one of the largest black rhinoceroses
ever seen
huge monster
leviathan rhinoceros
great unicorn
Rhinoceros-ship

perhaps the only opportunity
of ever beholding
a FULL-GROWN LIVING RHINOCEROS
in the United States

the public will please remember
there will be no additional charge
to see this extraordinary
curiosity

## GREAT FAMILY OF GIANTS

Giant Ox
weight 4,000 pounds
Giant Horse
22 hands high
Giant Ostrich
10 feet high
Giant Sea Lion
big as a cow
Giant Rhinoceros
larger than any two ever captured
Giant Camels
towering pyramids of the desert
Chang the Chinese Giant
tallest man in the world

hy Carlo Salome Victoria Mogur Old Bill Dit
etel Hans Kali Hash Harry Bomba Pharaoh C
her Gus Mohan Chiquita Kenya Kifaru Suze
nnie Clyde Max Rudy Heinz Patsy Young Joe
key Archibaldo III Isis Dimples Pongo Arun
to Pepe Ronald Sneha Thelma Chippie Deepa
logo Ringo Squeaker Thombotini Beulah Zulu
nrietta Pinoccio Tiny Twinkletoes Tytan Bogoc
b Wally Momela Padma Rowena Snoopy Ku
ssius Eva Floozie Fred Geraldine Helga Ian
iba Sherman Shuster Simon Tessie Bheema C
bo Marius Murray Pendula Phoebe Pixie Punc
nca Buck Buffy Bull Clic-Clic Daisy Mae
ria Angelica Martini Maybelle Mule Oscar Pop
dget Bumper Esperanza Igor Katie
oter Adolph Balthasar Big-B Bruno

**BY
ANY**

i Longhorn Marvin Mondo Nabob
l Rodney Spook Studley Stumpy Wrinkles Ba
rbert Pinky Sudan Brutus Hamish Kitty Mach
oba Elvira Puu Roberto Smudla Vijay Zero
urchill Cornelius Doc Eugene Gloria Milton Os
rmy Terai Thumper Tonka Baringo Franklin M
dir Petra Tron Ellora Elmer Mabel Mimi
mothi Rover Watson Zoe Blackstone Godot G
n Betty Boop Juniper Little Joe Priscilla Sagan
r Thor Veronica Barakas Bender Gemstone Klau
dley Poncho Whoopi Belur Boy Emmi Howell
k Steady Rosetta Stone Yvonne Zambezi Bagus
rmin' Norman Axl Donkey Equinox Kwanzaa
ari Tucker Ebony Gologob Independence Jaffna

aggie Ruby Felix Stamper Yard Nepal? Fritz
ed Lucy Oldeani Rosie Rupert Gunda Georgie-
Chloë Ferdinand Matilda Coco François Joseph
sha Rani Roughskin Stonewall Dinka Lulu C
Dolly Hatari Jake Mildred Momba Rufus J
vey Juliette Romeo Wooly Aphrodite Faith Ma
Cher Sonny Herman Jaypuri Toto Arthur Gar
Dublo Lady Leroy Pompey Reginald Roy St
Rudolph Shorty Tobias Arabella Bernadine Ber
Maggot Myrtle Notch Ear Oliveoil Panzer Prin
Delilah Fodder Jack Jemima Karoo King Kris
esh Roopa Samson Twink Willem Aggi Alice B
a Edith Ann Felicia Flossy Grunt Horace Lur
nestone Ralph Suki Winston Angalifu Beaureg

**OTHER** Lola Lucifer Moola Mungo Pas
**NAME** Cow Curly Daryll Frances Horte
Old Man Petite Pistol Poindexter Pr
lo Cody Deano Dynamite Embu Indira Mbo
aharajah Rocky Sanjoy Sweet Pea Arubarte Bala
n Casper Fatty Mack Rumi Shalom Atari Bu
Rommel Satan Scarface Shaboola Shiva Stonebre
Pandu Buzbie Debbie Freedom Hercules Johnst
x Rashmi Shy-Anne Cecil Daffodil Heidi Jo
Zimba Duke Moonstone Peggy Lee Wamba B
r Cleopatra Cyrano Gingabelle Henry Ollie Pee
ulinda Shah Spike Tatoo Augustina Bardia Brew
Jaunpur Marcelo Osupat Prakash Quinto Rapu
ynah Hailstone Ipak Kojak Namaste Nico S
Boo Dorothy Godavari Halloween Metro Qu
rgana Murphy Sauron Tex Tortoise Chitwan N

# THE FUN OF HUNTING THEM

I. Theodore Roosevelt, East Africa, 1910

*Any modern rifle is good enough. The determining factor is the man behind the gun*

I pushed forward the safety
of the double-barrelled Holland rifle
which I was now to use for the first time
on big game. Such a hard-hitting rifle
the best weapon for heavy game
I was using the Winchester
with full-jacketed bullets
I was anxious to try the sharp-pointed bullets
of the little Springfield rifle on him
I used all three of my rifles

*It would certainly be well if all killing of it were prohibited*

I fired for the chest
I fired hastily into the chest
I put the heavy bullet straight into its chest
I fired right and left into his body
I put in the right barrel
I struck him with my left-hand barrel
I again knocked it flat with the left-hand barrel
I put both barrels into and behind the shoulder
I fired into the shoulder again.
I fired into its flank both the bullets
remaining in my magazine
I emptied the magazine at his quarters and flank
I put in another heavy bullet
I had put nine bullets into him
I sent the bullet from the heavy Holland
just in front of her right shoulder
The bullet went through both lungs

It went through her vitals
My second bullet went in between
the neck and shoulder
The bullet entered between the neck and shoulder
and pierced his heart
The animal was badly hit
It needed two more bullets before it died
I had put in eight bullets, five from the Winchester
and three from the Holland

*To let the desire for 'record' heads become a craze is absurd*

None had decent horns
None with more than ordinary horns
None carried horns which made them worth shooting
It did not seem to have very good horns
Her horn was very poor
A poor horn
A stubby horn
A short, stubby, worn-down horn
His horn though fair was not remarkable
A fair horn
A good horn
The front horn measured fourteen inches
against his nineteen inches
It had good horns
The fore horn twenty-two inches long
the rear over seventeen
Thick horns of fair length
twenty-three and thirteen inches respectively
A stout horn, a little over two feet long
the girth at the base very great
A front horn nearly twenty-six inches long
His front horn was nearly twenty-nine inches long
He was a bull with a thirty-inch horn
A very fine specimen, with the front horn thirty-one inches long
much the longest horn of any of them

## II. King George V, Nepal, 1911

His Majesty displayed
that remarkable skill with the rifle
for which he has long been noted
among sportsmen
The King had an awkward shot at him
but missed. It was fired at and missed
by the King. It was a difficult shot for the King
who fired without apparent effect
There suddenly emerged
a fine bull rhinoceros. A solitary
bull rhinoceros suddenly appeared
before His Majesty
Only one rhinoceros was found
A cow with a well-grown calf was found
They happened upon two more
rhinoceroses
The King killed the first dead with one barrel
with his second wounded the other
The King again killed a rhinoceros
with a single shot. A second bullet
from His Majesty's rifle laid her stone dead
with a bullet through the chest
In due time it was dispatched
by His Majesty. It was eventually
killed by His Majesty

A wonderful day's sport
Such excellent sport
The sport was most successful

III. Ernest Hemingway, Tanzania, 1933

The first rhino
bustling short-leggedly
no reason ever to miss
almost too dark to shoot
I squeezed off
heard the *whonk* of the bullet
I *know* I hit him
a deep, moaning sort of groan
a blood-soaked sigh
on his side, dead
stroking the rhino's horn
measuring it with fingers spread
hide like vulcanized rubber
ears fringed with hair
tiny pig eyes
hell of an animal
how is his horn?
it isn't bad, nothing extra
the newly severed head of a rhino
twice the size of the one I'd killed
what is he? about thirty inches?
this rhino whose smaller horn was longer
than our big one
this huge, tear-eyed marvel of a rhino
it was like a kick in the stomach
why couldn't he just get a good one
two or three inches longer?
what a beautiful rhino
we had tried never to be competitive
I don't give a damn about these rhino
outside of the fun of hunting them
I'd like to get one
that wouldn't look silly
beside that dream rhino of his

OFFICIALS SAID

On Thursday    On Saturday    On Monday    On Friday
On Tuesday    On Wednesday    On Wednesday
In the wee hours of Wednesday
On Monday    On Monday night    Probably on Monday night
On Tuesday    On Tuesday morning    Around 11 AM on Tuesday
On Tuesday evening    At 8 PM on Tuesday
On Friday    In the early hours of Friday
On Saturday    On Saturday    On Saturday    In the wee hours of Saturday
On Saturday morning    On Saturday night    Late on Saturday
Earlier this week    Yesterday    Last night    Late last night
During the wee hours    At 1:45 AM    At 6:10 in the morning
This morning


a group of poachers    a group of five poachers    a group of about five poachers
a gang of poachers    a gang of five to six poachers    an organized gang of poachers
an armed gang    heavily armed poachers    three heavily armed poachers
armed militants equipped with sophisticated weapons
a group of poachers with sophisticated weapons
armed with assault rifles    armed with AK-47s
and double-barrelled guns


attacked    shot at    fired at    opened fire on    gunned down    shot dead    killed
killed    killed    killed    killed    killed    killed    killed    killed    killed    killed


a one-horned rhino    a rare one-horned rhino
another one-horned rhino    yet another one-horned rhino
an adult rhino    a male rhino    an adult male rhino
a female rhino    one more mature female rhino
a translocated female rhino    a rhino calf
two rhinos    another two rhinos
a third rhino    four rhinos
another rhino    another rhino    another rhino    another rhino    another rhino
yet another rhino

and sawed off     cut off     chopped off     hacked off   gouged out     extracted
its horn     chopped off a horn from a live rhino
were able to chop away the horn of one
took away its horn
decamped with its horn
fled with the horn
fled with three horns
managed to flee with their horns

in about 15 minutes only

## GOING, GOING, GONE

Lot 1
Small bird-form rhinoceros horn cup, 17$^{th}$ century

Lot 2
Rhinoceros horn libation cup with magnolia in fitted wooden
    stand, late 17$^{th}$ century
The base has a magnolia bud broken off and reaffixed with glue
    adhesive

Lot 3
Rhinoceros horn cup, 17$^{th}$/18$^{th}$ century
A chip to the tip of the tail of the dragon climbing up the exterior
    spout and a chip to the leg of the dragon on the handle
Scattered filled holes from insect activity

Lot 4
Extremely rare and exquisitely carved eight stallions rhinoceros horn
    libation cup
A few cracks at the rim and a few gouges to the inner surface just
    above the handle

Lot 5
Rare and superbly carved lotus-leaf shaped rhinoceros horn water
    dropper

Lot 6
George III silver and rhinoceros horn handled punch ladle

Lot 7
Ottoman sword with rhinoceros horn grip

Lot 8
Translucent rhinoceros horn hilt dagger with silver mounts, late
    19$^{th}$ century

Lot 9
Rhinoceros horn hilted dagger with scabbard, turn of the 20<sup>th</sup> century
Scabbard covered in black velvet with silver mountings

Lot 10
Victorian rhinoceros horn swagger stick

Lot 11
Edwardian silver mounted rhinoceros horn riding crop

Lot 12
Western walking cane with rhinoceros horn handle, 19<sup>th</sup> century
The handle carved in low relief with two horse riders in western garments racing towards the finish line, the stick made of lightweight hardwood

Lot 13
Rhinoceros horn handle dress cane, late 19<sup>th</sup> century
Body mud-brown, handle n-shaped in a dark brown colour
Worn from use

Lot 14
Two rhinoceros horn cosmetic jars with covers, c.1920

Lot 15
A row of fifty-five graduated oval rhinoceros horn beads

Lot 16
Rhinoceros horn ashtray and lighter

Lot 17
Bronze-mounted rhinoceros foot humidor

Lot 18
Taxidermied rhinoceros foot container with turned oak rim, early 20<sup>th</sup> century

Lot 19
Stuffed and mounted rhinoceros foot with mahogany lid

Lot 20
A pair of rhinoceros horns mounted on a wooden plinth

# CONSERVATION

## I.

Almost 50 animals among extinction efforts greatest hunted increase is more of our rhinoceroses since southern this time than their 14,000 success stories short savannas protected population of numbers law inhabited international grass discovered currently by 1895 Africa

## II.

Anti-poaching alone but dramatically equip for horn however illegal implement increase killed 1800s laws medicinal need no number over 1,000 patrols poaching saved species successes train this tougher value was touted thought scientific story provide public needed late idea increasing from 2007 continues animal awareness

## CLARA'S FAVOURITE TIPPLE

A bowl of beer above deck aboard ship
or wine, a carafe al fresco
She'll settle for port especially
if listing to starboard
But she's on the wagon now
can't afford the hangovers
She's clumsy at the best of times
slipping, smashing dishes
rhino in a china shop
Best to go teetotal

## CLARA INCOGNITO

She dons a mask of silk and lace
disappears into the streets of Venice
consorts with smugglers, thieves
card sharks in coffeehouses
Patricians and plebs switch places
now she's doing the looking
The mask commands respect
no one recognizes her
not even the agent
taking notes in the corner

## CLARA THE COLLECTOR

She assembles a menagerie
of her own: curios, porcelain
small skeletons, the eggs
of rare birds. She treads carefully
between the cabinets
odd toes clicking
against the tiles. A tilt
a crash—the weight
of her collection
could crush her

## CLARA DELIGHTS IN HER STATUS AS MUSE

She lies on her left side, sleeps, leaps
saucy, insouciant, somnolent
rhinoceros! Picasso can't make her
stranger, reshuffling her into a bull
She goes head to head with Dali
outshines Warhol's silk
She's a blank canvas
rolling around in paint
out Pollocks Pollock
puts her body into it

## CLARA INSPIRES THE SCRIBES

O rhinoceros! who dares to name thee?
Rhinoceros of all rhinoceroses
A rhinoceros by any other name
would be as fleet
A rhinoceros is a rhinoceros is a rhinoceros
You, of course, are a rhinoceros
but were always a rhinoceros
*Hooray*, say the rhinoceroses
Every rhinoceros has its horn
unless it doesn't

## CLARA CANARY GIRL

She butts out her cigarette
pulls on overalls, overshoes, and cap
takes her place on the line
at the shell-filling factory, enjoys
free tea and biscuits in the canteen
Her thick skin takes on a yellowish hue
and her hair, well, she's always wanted
to be a redhead. Better to be
behind the man behind the gun
than in front of him

## CLARA IS READY FOR HER CLOSE-UP

She's played opposite John Wayne
who couldn't keep up even in a jeep
and under Johnny Weissmuller
whose thighs still chafe at the memory
She chafes at being upstaged
by Maureen O'Sullivan, Elsa Martinelli
and a trio of baby elephants. Her star turn
comes playing a metaphor for Fellini
A ship rides low with a lovesick
rhinoceros in its belly

## CLARA JOINS THE SECRETARIAL POOL

She seeks counsel on the crucial question
of nylons, hers bunch at the knees
she can't keep the seams straight
A co-worker shares a wartime trick:
go bare-legged, draw a perfect line
with eye pencil up the back of each
Her vision is poor but her hearing acute
She takes dictation like a pro
grinds her teeth nights
like any beast in captivity

## CLARA GOES TO LAW SCHOOL

She learns about *habeus corpus*
*res ipsa loquitur, damnum absque*
*injuria*, becomes committed
to environmental protection
and animal rights. She dances
a tap dance in the student revue
She's happiest flipping
through law reports late
in the library, glasses fixed firmly
on the end of her nose

## CLARA IN SPACE

She feels a tug at her ankles
yet she's weightless. It's upside-down
aerial ballet. She mightn't
have run away from the circus
if she'd had a turn on the trapeze
She's heard of the dog
in endless orbit
but isn't worried, skywrites
a message: wander alone
like a rhinoceros

A number of the poems in this collection borrow fragments of text from a variety of sources. The specifics are detailed below. I'd also like to acknowledge three books that were enormously helpful to me in learning about rhinoceroses in general and Clara in particular: T.H. Clarke's *The Rhinoceros from Dürer to Stubbs, 1515–1799*; L.C. Rookmaaker's *The Rhinoceros in Captivity*; and Glynis Ridley's *Clara's Grand Tour: Travels with a Rhinoceros in Eighteenth-Century Europe*.

### A Natural History of the Rhinoceros
Fragments of text borrowed from: Ctesias, *Ancient India*; Oppian, *Kynegetika*; Pliny, *The Natural History*; Kosmas Indikopleustes, *De Mundo*; Marco Polo, *The Travels of Marco Polo*; Valentin Ferdinand, *Letter*; Edward Topsell, *The History of Four-Footed Beasts and Serpents*; James Bontius, *An Account of the Diseases, Natural History, and Medicines of the East Indies*; John Evelyn, *The Diary of John Evelyn*; I. Parsons, *A Letter from Dr. Parsons to Martin Folkes, President of the Royal Society, containing the Natural History of the Rhinoceros*; L'Abbe Ladvocat, *Letter on the Rhinoceros to a Member of the Royal Society of London*; Comte de Buffon, *Natural History*; Oliver Goldsmith, *A History of the Earth and Animated Nature*.

### Elephant v. Rhinoceros
Fragments of text borrowed from: Ctesias, *Ancient India*; Diodorus Siculus, *Bibliotheca Historica*; Oppian, *Kynegetika*; Pliny, *The Natural History*; Valentin Ferdinand, *Letter*; Guillaume de Salluste du Bartas, *La Semaine*; Jean Chardin, *Travels in Persia*; Edward Topsell, *The History of Four-Footed Beasts and Serpents*; *Arabian Nights*; Comte de Buffon, *Natural History*; George Anson, *A Voyage Around the World*; Oliver Goldsmith, *A History of the Earth and Animated Nature*; Thomas Williamson, *Oriental Field Sports*; John Church, *A Cabinet of Quadrupeds*; Richard Owen, *On the Anatomy of the Indian Rhinoceros*.

### According to the Apothecary
Fragments of text borrowed from the writings of St. Hildegard of Bingen and a seventeenth-century London physician's advertisement. On the medicinal claims that have been made about unicorn and rhinoceros horns respectively, Odell Shepard's *Lore of the Unicorn*, and Richard Ellis's *Tiger Bone & Rhino Horn* were particularly helpful.

### Rhinoceros Odyssey
Passages in italics are quotations from accounts (or translations thereof) that appeared in handbills, broadsides, newspapers, letters, and diaries during Clara's lifetime.

**Magrath the Giant and the Rhinoceros**
The title of this poem is taken from a painting by Pietro Longhi. Fragments of text borrowed from: D.J. Cunningham, *The Skeleton of the Irish Giant, Cornelius Magrath*; H.R. Swanzy, *Note on Defective Vision and Other Ocular Derangements in Cornelius Magrath, The Irish Giant*; Edward J. Wood, *Giants and Dwarfs*; and articles that appeared in various newspapers during the lifetime of Cornelius Magrath.

**The Wild Beast Men**
Passages in italics are quotations from advertisements, newspapers articles, and letters that were written during the subjects' lifetimes or obituaries published shortly after their deaths.

**O'Brien's Four Shows**
Fragments of text borrowed from *Guidebook to O'Brien's Four Shows Consolidated*.

**Great Family of Giants**
This is a found poem, with all of the text taken from a single nineteenth-century circus poster.

**The Fun of Hunting Them**
Fragments of text borrowed from: Theodore Roosevelt, *African Game Trails: An Account of the African Wanderings of an American Hunter-Naturalist*; *The Historic Record of the Imperial Visit to India, 1911*; and Ernest Hemingway, *Green Hills of Africa*.

**Officials Said**
Fragments of text borrowed from newspaper reports of poaching incidents that occurred in 2013 in national parks in the Indian state of Assam.

**Going, Going, Gone**
Descriptions borrowed from the listings of several online auction sites.

**Clara Inspires the Scribes**
Lines borrowed and adapted from Elizabeth Barrett Browning, W.B. Yeats, William Shakespeare, Gertrude Stein, Robert Frost, Charles Bukowski, and Poison.

**Clara Goes to Law School**
This poem is inspired by Franz Kafka's "The New Advocate."

**Clara in Space**
The final message attributed to Clara here is taken from a very early Buddhist text known as the Rhinoceros Sutra. Remnants of a 2000-year-old birchbark scroll upon which the entire text once appeared are housed in the British Library (the national library of the United Kingdom).

## ACKNOWLEDGEMENTS

Thanks to Jennifer LoveGrove in whose company I first encountered Clara the rhinoceros at an exhibition of ceramic animals at the Gardiner Museum.

Thanks to Jay MillAr and to my fellow participants in the iteration of his Long Poem Workshop in which my rhinoceros obsession began to take poetic form.

Thanks to Hoa Nguyen and Stuart Ross, who have been generous mentors as I shifted from writing fiction to poetry.

Thanks again to Jay and to Hazel Millar and the rest of the BookThug team for shepherding this book to publication.

Thanks to my mom and dad, who continue to be enormously supportive of all of my literary endeavours.

And thanks to Eric Bridenbaker, who was a most encouraging first reader, and who very patiently accompanied me on various rhinoceros-related quests during recent trips to London, New York, and Washington, DC. This book is for you, Eric.

Earlier versions of some of the poems in this book have appeared in *This Magazine*, *Lemon Hound*, *The Puritan*, and *NewPoetry*.

**KATE SUTHERLAND** was born in Scotland, grew up in Saskatchewan, and now lives in Toronto, where she is a professor at Osgoode Hall Law School. She is the author of two collections of short stories: *Summer Reading* (winner of a Saskatchewan Book Award for Best First Book) and *All In Together Girls. How to Draw a Rhinoceros* is her first book of poems.

Manufactured as the First Edition of
*How to Draw a Rhinoceros* in the Fall of 2016
by BookThug.

Distributed in Canada by the Literary Press Group:
www.lpg.ca

Distributed in the US by Small Press Distribution:
www.spdbooks.org

Shop online at www.bookthug.ca

BOOK
PRODUCTION
WAR ECONOMY
STANDARD

Edited for the press by Phil Hall
Type + design by Kate Hargreaves
Copy edited by Ruth Zuchter